D1824415

Pocket Guide To Writing Profit-Boosting Sales Letters...

A manager's guide to the secrets behind the stunningly persuasive words millionaire marketers use to turn passive readers into eager and profitable customers!

by Carol A E Bentley

Published by Sarceaux Publications
ISBN 978 0 9549206 4 3

Cover Design by Millennium Design Group, Inc. www.millworldwide.com
© Carol A E Bentley & Bob D'Amico

Carol A E Bentley has asserted her rights, under the Copyright, Design
and Patents Act 1988, to be identified as the author of this work.

Copyright © 2009 by Carol A E Bentley

All rights reserved by the author. No part of this publication may be
reproduced or transmitted in any form or by any means, electronic or
mechanical, including photocopying, recording, or any information storage
and retrieval system, without permission in writing from the publishers.

All trademarks and copyrights acknowledged.

This book is offered as information only. Although every precaution has
been taken in its preparation, the author assumes no responsibility for
errors or omissions. Neither is any liability assumed for damages resulting
from the use of the information contained herein.

Catalogue Data
Bentley, Carol A. E.
Pocket Guide To Writing Profit-Boosting Sales Letters
1. Copywriting 2. Marketing 3. Direct Response Marketing

Carol Bentley specialises in copywriting for businesses, including direct
mail, direct response adverts, web page copy, email marketing, 'white
papers' and short guides. Visit **www.businesswriting4u.co.uk** for details.

To enquire about having Carol work on your current or next copywriting
project or to engage her to speak at your next conference, call her office
on +44 1929 423411 or email office@businesswriting4u.co.uk

You can also write to her c/o Sarceaux Publications, 104 Victoria Avenue,
Swanage, Dorset, BH19 1AS UK

Carol is the author of 'I Want To Buy Your Product.. Have You Sent Me A
Letter Yet?' and 'Beat The Recession: Proven Marketing Tactics'. Both
books are rated 5* on Amazon.

Table of Contents

INTRODUCTION

Have you noticed how some businesses seem to be ultra-successful? Even as others fail?

Why is that?

The answer is simple; they have three crucial things in place:

- A great product/service that fulfils a hungry market's demands

- A clear understanding of their target market

- Powerful, effective marketing strategies and action plans

And they use powerful marketing secrets to generate more and more business. They recognise the importance of nurturing their prospects and customers – and one of the ways they do this is through their communication.

> "Instead of a paltry result most companies, with small changes to what they are saying in their marketing, can gain significant improvements without spending a single penny more"

First off - they make sure all their marketing

messages are crystal clear <u>and</u> informative so their prospect and client always feels valued and respected. It is a crucial part of any successful marketing strategy. And it's one you can easily use too.

But, there are so many marketing messages you have to compete against it is difficult to make sure yours stands out from the rest. And, when you do get enquiries or orders, you need to know which marketing message has worked... and why... so you can repeat it.

There's a Science to Writing Powerful Sales Messages...

Many people do not realise there is a science to writing a sales message that generates measurable results, whether it goes out in a letter or on a website; in an advert or in a brochure. It is a formula that exponentially increases your chances of getting the reaction you want - and it is easy to learn and use.

<u>Powerful headlines; persuasive words and, where appropriate, relevant pictures - with captions - makes all the difference to the result you get.</u>

Having studied many different marketing gurus and putting into practice, in my business and my clients' businesses, the skills I've gained I have accumulated a world of insight and experience into how sales messages can be written to succeed – instead of failing. And you can do it too... with a little bit of insight and guidance and that's what this pocket guide delivers.

Do you agree that your sales message must achieve

these three things?

1. Seize your prospect's attention. If you do not 'stop him in his tracks' so he takes note of what you are saying you won't get a result, will you?

2. Sustain his interest by focusing on what he gets out of using your product / service.

3. Act as the catalyst to action. If your reader does not take favourable action then your sales message has failed and you've wasted your time and - potentially - your money.

In this guide the sequence of 7 steps concentrates on writing sales messages.

Although I'll talk specifically about sales letters - keep in mind all these insider tips can be used in **any** sales message; online or offline.

I'll reveal how to turn your sales letter into a revenue generating machine using some of the secrets the millionaire marketers use every day to stay at the top of their game. You discover...

☑ how to seize attention with your headlines;

☑ how to make sure you keep your prospect's interest;

☑ what your letter should contain;

☑ the structure you should incorporate in any letter to generate the best possible result for you;

☑ how to make sure *your reader takes the action* you want.

This can only happen if the person is interested in what you've got to offer – so the other important aspect, as I've already mentioned, is understanding how to target the right people.

Keep an open mind because every nuance; every insider tip I reveal - as I've already said -can be used in all your marketing communication... not just sales letters!

Kind regards

Carol Bentley

Author of 'I Want To Buy Your Product... Have You Sent Me A Letter Yet?' and 'Beat The Recession: Proven Marketing Tactics'.

STEP 1: DISCOVER YOUR MOST RESPONSIVE MARKET...

Before you can write your sales letter, you have to know who you are writing to. If you write to the wrong people or businesses you might just as well flush your hard-won marketing budget down the drain.

Many businesses tend to send out letters to people they think are interested in what they had to offer. You have probably heard the normal response to any bulk mailing like this in business ranges from 0.5% to 1% - any more is regarded as a very good result.

This is usually because the letters are sent to a list of unqualified names/contacts. That is like taking a handful of seed and scattering them on the ground and hoping some will take root, before being eaten by the birds.

'Preparing The Ground'

You have to 'sow' your seeds in prepared ground and nurture them to increase the chances of healthy growth. The same applies to the sales messages you send out.

Target, Aim, Fire...

[CASE STUDY] One of my clients, who owned a letting management agency, wanted to offer his services to the people buying apartments at a new, salubrious development. This was the first project I had discussed with him and he showed me the letter he was planning to send out to introduce his services. The letter was very formal and rather dull.

After some discussion he agreed I should write the sales letter for him. In my letter I concentrated on what the client would receive; peace of mind; the assurance their property would be handled properly and all the benefits they would gain by letting their property and, more importantly, by letting it through my client (the letter is shown in its entirety in my book 'I Want To Buy Your Product... Have You Sent Me A Letter Yet?' in which I expand more on these sales writing techniques).

We sent the letter to the people who had already agreed to buy an apartment – this was a very small and very targeted list.

The letter went out the week before Christmas; I felt our prospects would possibly get bored in the long break between Christmas and New Year and would read the letter, even though it was four pages long... some people would regard that as too long.

We had 2 responses between Christmas and New Year.

We then sent a slightly shorter follow-up message after New Year reminding them about our first letter and giving them the essence of the offer again.

The final response from this targeted audience was 44.2%. My client offered a very professional and personal service and he was able to convert 63.16% of those responses into actual clients.

(This amazingly high rate of response and conversion is extremely unusual – a percentage of 1% - 2% would normally be regarded as an excellent outcome. But it does show how precise targeting can boost your results dramatically).

So, making sure of your target audience and preparing properly is crucial to your success.

'Preparing' for your mailing campaign means identifying people / businesses who have already bought / expressed an interest in what you have to offer.

How To Identify Who To Write To...

It depends upon where your prospects' details come from in the first place. If they are in your database; one you have spent time building from the customers and prospects you have had over the years, then you will have made a note of what would interest them - *haven't you?*

Of course, if your business is a new venture or you're moving into a new market, then you don't have that database and you need to get people to qualify themselves by responding to an offer.

Let's say you have rented a mailing list of 2000 addresses. You qualified as much as you could when you sourced the list; types of business, contacts within the business, geographical location etc. or specific individuals in the location or demographic group you want to target.

Ideally you would prefer a list that specifically identifies those businesses or individuals who have bought/enquired about similar items to what you offer. Sometimes you can do this with consumer mailing lists - individuals – but, for businesses, that information is rarely available to you.

So you need to qualify your purchased list and the only way you're going to do it is by getting the contacts to *tell you* they are interested.

How Do I Find People Interested In What I Offer?

By offering something that elicits a response and so clearly identifies their interest.

It could be a FREE report on something that interests your prospect and is connected with your main product or service (as this pocket guide you are reading does). Frequently asked questions and your expert answers make a good give-away; or 10 Little Known Tips on... or a recorded & transcribed interview with an industry expert (or getting someone to interview *you* as the expert) can have high perceived value for your prospect.

If you're aiming to get people to attend a seminar then a FREE or low cost taster session, teleconference or webinar may be the right 'carrot' to entice your prospects.

The key is to get people to self qualify themselves for your main product/service by responding to your related offer.

Crucial: You must write your letter in a way that grabs their attention and entices them to take up what you are offering.

The structure of your message - whether it is by email, letter, advert or even telephone; whether it is to entice or give the main offer - should always start with a powerful headline or opening sentence; a strong one that appeals to them.

But the most important thing to remember when creating your headline or opening sentence is that what interests **you** may not attract your audience. A strong headline for you may not create even the slightest ripple of attention from others – and what appeals to them may have no substance in your eyes.

Test Your Headline Writing Skills...

Take a look at some adverts or marketing letters you have seen or received; preferably ones that have appealed to you. Think about what attracted you to the headline.

Now - following a similar style; write 4 or 5 headlines for your product / service you think will work. Ask 4 or 5 people, preferably not family or close friends, to place the headlines in the order that appeals to them.

I think you will find it is highly unlikely everyone will have placed them in the same order - you may even find their preferences are the complete opposite to yours!

This is why you should not be satisfied with the first headline you think of. And when you *have* found a few headlines that seem to make sense, you should still test, test and test again.

In fact you should test by sending letters with different headlines out to a sample of your 'database' before mailing to your whole list. And then, for your main campaign, use the one that received the highest response.

Because headlines are so crucial to the success of any marketing message you put out, I'm going to concentrate on how to write eye-catching headlines in the next section.

I'll share with you some of the most powerful words you can have in your headline... *but you must only use these if you want your headlines to sell.*

Until then... have a think about what you could offer to your prospects that they would find valuable and would clearly indicate their serious interest in your main product or service.

STEP 2:
HARNESS INCREDIBLE
HEADLINE POWER...

In the previous step I invited you to write a few headlines for your business and ask your colleagues to rate their appeal.

How did you get on?

Did you discover - as I suggested - that people had different views? And that's just from a few readers. Imagine the disparity when you put those headlines in front of your prospective customers!

This is why most marketing gurus tell you, to write as many headlines as possible before selecting one for your marketing message – up to 100 is suggested by many experts.

When I first heard this my reaction was probably the same as yours is now – "*How*? Writing 2 or 3 is enough of a struggle, how can I possibly write 100!"

Well, as with any large project you create a system and break it into smaller tasks.

Be creative and brainstorm with colleagues – let them act as a catalyst for you. *Oh, and by the way, don't go for 'clever, but obscure' headlines* – leave that to the larger organisations who can afford to waste their money on entertaining mailing campaigns or adverts.

There are many proven response words that, when used in headlines, increase the chance of your letter attracting people enough to read further.

Writing a number of headlines for each of these soon gives you 100 headlines. So, by breaking your tasks into just a few headlines for each response word, it doesn't seem anywhere near as daunting as thinking of writing 100 immediately, does it?

Your headline should 'shout' out what your offer is – as I said before, don't be obscure or 'clever'. If your reader has to think about what you mean they're not going to bother with it and they certainly won't be encouraged to read the rest of your letter.

Describe a real benefit, as this headline does...

'New System Guarantees You Will Lose Weight Permanently

– Or Your Money Back'

In an advert this could be shortened to...

"Guaranteed, Permanent Weight Loss"

However, in both cases this is a 'general claim' headline that is probably the same as what many other companies say. Neither of them really grabs attention.

Be specific and your headline is not only noticed it becomes more believable. Don't worry if your headline for your letter is long – if you are saying something your reader has a keen interest in the length is not relevant...

"New system guarantees you lose at least 10lbs in weight within 28 days, without exercising or starving yourself, and what's more it is permanent – or you can have your money back"

If you are using a headline, make sure it is big and bold.

Occasionally you may decide it is not appropriate to use a very large headline at the top of your letter; if you are writing to more reserved professionals like accountants or solicitors, in which case you must make absolutely sure your first sentence is riveting for your reader.

11 Proven Response Power Words:

Earlier I mentioned response words are powerful eye-catchers that attract people to your letter. When used effectively within your headline it draws your prospect into your letter.

Remember, the whole purpose of your headline is to get your prospect to read the first paragraph of your letter, which in turn leads them onto the next paragraph and so on.

There are hundreds of these power words that have been tested and proven to work. Here are a few for you to try out...

You / Your – People are interested, primarily, in anything that helps them, makes their life easier or more enjoyable. Including the word You / Your catches their attention. In this headline the specific value of the income also attracts interest.

> **"Your Investment in Pinesuites**
> **Development Could Be Worth Up To**
> **£12,960 per Year in Income"**

These - This is a very famous headline that has worked for many years. It is a curiosity headline; the reader wants to know what <u>these</u> mistakes are and if they make them. If the word 'these' had been left out the headline would not have got the high response it did (and continues to get).

> **"Do You Make These Mistakes In English?"**

Who Else – this is using the 'me too' principle. The offer implies someone else has already benefited and your reader could as well.

> **"Who Else Wants To Lose 10lbs In 28 Days?"**

Which – using 'which' in a headline also creates curiosity – part of what makes us human is our curiosity. If the headline is asking a question that intrigues your reader they want to know more. In this advert using the word 'which' gets the reader to automatically consider they may have a skin problem they could get rid of.

> **"Five Familiar Skin Troubles – Which Do**
> **You Want To Overcome?"**

Now – implies that 'at last' here is something

worthwhile or beneficial for the reader.

"Now You <u>Can</u> Get a Business Loan – Even If Your Bank Has Turned You Down"

New – always a good word to use – provided what you are offering *is* new. People like new things, ideas and innovation. With a 'new offer' your existing customer is encouraged to spend more with you.

"New Innovative System Reduces Computer Downtime"

Bargain – everyone likes a bargain. We all like to think we have got a brilliant deal; 'A bargain'.

"Fantastic Bargain, 3-in-1 Business Seminar at a Massively Reduced Price"

Free – although many people think this word is overused, it still attracts attention. Even though we all tend to believe that there is 'no such thing as a free lunch' we are still intrigued by the possibility of receiving something without any cost to us.

"Free Report Reveals Secrets of Marketing Experts"

How / How to – using these words implies education and information. Finding out 'how to' do or get something or 'how' something affected an outcome attracts anyone who likes to know more about what is going on. Tying this with a problem your reader may have makes it even more effective.

"How to Have a Cool, Quiet Bedroom – Even on Hot Nights"

Hurry – creates a sense of urgency, especially if it ties in with a 'bargain' or time limited offer.

"Hurry, get your free copy before stocks run out"

"Hurry this drastically reduced offer is only available for 10 days"

Breakthrough – implies that whatever is offered is at the 'cutting-edge' and therefore your reader would be amongst the first to benefit from the service or product.

"Breakthrough Business Seminar Gives You Key Pointers on Marketing, Commercial Funding and Handling Business Growth Effectively"

As I said previously, there are many more – look at any marketing mail you receive or any adverts that catch your attention – what attracted you?

Would other people react in the same way?

Could you adopt and adapt the essence of the headline for your service or product?

It's surprising; I've often found the real headline gems appear in the last 20 headlines! If I'd only written 2 or 3, they would never have materialised. This is why writing as many headlines as you can is a good investment of your time because, once it is done, it serves you for many years to come in your business.

If the idea of sitting down to write 100 headlines, even with these power words, is daunting you could make it easier and decide to write a set number of headlines on each day of the week – if you write just 5 headlines per day – at the end of a week you have your 25+ headlines. And within a few weeks you'll reach your 100 target.

The beauty of doing it this way is you probably won't get frustrated with a mental block and, by now, some of your headlines will really sparkle at you.

By the way, as you create your headlines you will find that whilst 2 or 3 really stand out, others are a natural follow-on for sub headings you can use within your letter or as a P.S.

And sometimes you'll find it sensible to combine 2 good headlines into 1 powerful statement – as I did with...

"Find Out How You Can Avoid up to £20,000 in Fines

...Important Advice on Legal Issues for Letting Agents"

Your Turn...

Using the examples I've given as a guide, write headlines for your business; write at least 2 for each response word.

Jot them down now and don't continue reading until you have completed this exercise:

You / Your: _____

_____

_____

Who Else:

_____

_____

_____

Which:

_____

_____

_____

Now:

_____

_____

_____

New:

_____

_____

_____

_____

Bargain:

_____

_____

_____

_____

_____

_____

Free: _____

_____

_____

_____

How / How to: _____

_____

_____

_____

Hurry: _____

_____

_____

_____

Breakthrough: _____

_____

_____

Finished?

Congratulations! – You have just written 20 headlines for your business!

Don't stop there... repeat the exercise until you have 100 to select your best efforts from.

In the next step we'll take a look at the content in your sales message; what you write, *the words you use* has a major impact on your results... until then, good luck with writing your sales-winning headlines.

STEP 3:
MAKE YOUR SALES
LETTER COMPELLING...

The most difficult - and probably stressful - part of your sales message you need to get right is your headline. You probably realised that as you went through the previous step.

Many professional copywriters use the majority of their time to craft a winning headline. Simply because, without a powerful headline, the rest of the sales message is unlikely to be read.

So, now you've completed the hardest part of your letter, you will find that writing your letter to go with your headline is so much easier because it focuses your mind on what you want to tell your reader.

First of all, let me dispel a myth about direct response sales messages (a direct response message is a sales letter /advert/webpage intended to elicit an action from your reader) – **short is <u>not</u> necessarily best**.

> **"The more you tell (factually) the more you sell"**
> *John Caples*

If the person you are writing to is attracted to your offer they want to know as much as possible about it so they can make an informed decision. If your message does not give your reader enough details – so they are confident about buying from you – you won't get a qualified response.

You see, a short letter containing a minimum number of words is like putting a gag on your best sales person 30 seconds after they get to an appointment with an important prospect.

You wouldn't stop your salesperson explaining about your product / service; the benefits the prospect would gain and how you would deliver their order, would you?

In fact, I'd bet you expect your salesperson to demonstrate how effective your service / product is; the benefits the prospect could expect to receive and why your company is the best supplier.

That's true, isn't it?

This is the same job your letter is supposed to do...

> *In 1905 John E. Kennedy told Albert I. Thomas that advertising is 'Salesmanship in Print'*

Now in modern technology, especially if you are using the Internet to reach your customers, you may see shorter text messages accompanied by video or audio tracks. In a letter, you don't have that advantage so everything you would include in those additional sound and visual tracks needs to be included in your written letter.

If you want to know what to put in your letter

listen to what your best salesperson is saying. If s/he can persuade people to buy your product/service – ethically – then so will your letter if you use the same explanations and informative descriptions.

Please remember <u>every</u> letter you write should be your 'salesperson in print' and should give the full story at all times.

Think about it for a moment - the last time you made a major purchase – did you take the time to find out as much as you could about the reliability and suitability of the product or service <u>before</u> making a decision?

I recall a while ago when my husband wanted to buy a cinema 'surround' sound and DVD system, he spent *hours* pouring over reviews, internet information, specification details, comparing one make to another and then one model to another before he made his final choice. <u>*Then*</u> he took time to consider the supplier he would use, making sure they were reliable and able to supply in an acceptable timescale.

You may think "Well if you are spending a lot of money of course you take these precautions" – however, he was spending less than £1,000 at the time, but he still wanted to know everything he could find out, so he could make an informed decision he would not regret afterwards.

I'm glad to say all his research paid off. We bought a very good system we thoroughly enjoyed and the supplier delivered it very quickly, as promised.

Supply <u>All</u> The Facts And Figures – Good <u>And</u> Bad

Be honest with your prospect. When you approach him you can make life so much easier for him by supplying <u>all</u> the facts and figures, <u>all</u> the details he needs – good <u>and</u> bad. After all, we all know it is better to buy something with your eyes wide open.

By telling your prospect the 'not so good' stuff he'll feel more confident about believing the beneficial details you describe.

So, if it takes 2, 3, 16 or even more pages in a letter to explain the offer; the benefits; the downside of not taking it, what it is not suitable for and all other relevant information, that is what you should do.

The only 'cardinal sin' is if you make your letter very boring. That is unforgivable!

Avoiding a Boring Letter...

<u>So how do you avoid writing a boring letter?</u> Surely if it is all facts and figures it's going to be tedious for your reader – except for the few people who like excessive detail?

A boring letter is a trap you must avoid at all costs and it's very easy to do this.

Think about the people you are communicating with and make sure you use the right language – don't be 'pompous' or over formal. Write your letter as if you were holding a conversation with someone, be enthusiastic and...

Practise Writing 'As You Speak'

Your letter comes over as more natural and easier to read when you 'write as you would speak'. It is one time when knowing all the English Grammar rules could be a disadvantage. Listen to any conversation and you'll notice that people rarely worry about using full sentences with correct grammar. You hear exclamations and short responses to what someone else has said, as well as normal sentences.

If you find it difficult to 'write as you would speak' because you were educated to write properly, with the correct grammar and in full sentences, then try this little trick:

Record yourself describing your product or service to a close friend, with all the enthusiasm you can muster. Then transcribe the conversation and use that as the base of your letter.

Use Stories & Testimonials...

Use stories and incidents to demonstrate how your product or service has benefited other people/companies. Explain the challenge/problem the other people faced before buying your service or product and what you did for them. For business purchases these are known as 'case-studies'.

Include testimonials from satisfied customers – not the usual 'excellent service, would recommend', make sure the testimonial tells what you did for your customer and, more importantly, what was the real benefit and result they received.

My client, the one I told you about earlier, wrote this testimonial for me...

> "It has been invaluable to have an expert writing targeted marketing material that has achieved such fantastic results – 44.2% response to a small mailing is amazing"
>
> *Martin Moore, Martin & Co, Poole*

Wherever possible it should also describe the problem they were facing.

In the next step in this sequence I reveal two crucial questions you must answer for your reader

- or risk failure.

But first, why not spend some time gathering together the testimonials your customers have given you and decide which ones to use in your next letter.

STEP 4:
TWO SACRED 'MUST-BE-OBEYED' COPYWRITING RULES

In the previous step I explained how using stories to demonstrate benefits is a powerful way to engage with your prospect. It is all tied in with answering the two most critical questions your prospect is asking.

> "The prospect doesn't give a damn about you, your company, or your product. All that matters is, 'What's in it for me?"
> Bob Hacker

If you don't answer these questions you are greatly reducing the number of responses your sales message might generate.

The two questions?

What's In It For Me (WIIFM) and **So What**?

It doesn't matter who you are writing to, every potential customer has these very important questions in mind...

'What's In It For Me?'

- Why should I bother to read this letter?

- What will I gain?

- What are the benefits of this offer?

• What problem does it solve for me?

If your letter starts off with a sentence stating how long you have been in business, the reaction from your audience might be '*So What?*'

Unless you turn that statement into a tangible benefit for the reader, it is probably of no interest to them.

Obviously if your prospect has already been in contact with you it may be appropriate to create or build confidence in your company by demonstrating its longevity. But in a first contact letter it is highly unlikely to be the most important aspect for them.

And, as you answer these questions, write your letter with your audience in mind. Change 'I's, 'my', 'mine', 'our', etc. to 'you', 'yours' – write the benefits from the reader's point of view – not from yours. And always remember to write as if you were writing to a single person. Even if you are sending the letter out to thousands of people, only one person is reading each individual copy.

If you are not used to writing letters in this way write your letter as normal, then go through and restructure the sentence describing real benefits for the reader.

Compare the difference between the following sample letters; A & B.

Sample letter A is an exact copy (except for the originator's name and company) of a letter I received.

The writing style is very formal and the emphasis

is on the person and the company sending the letter - no mention is made of any potential benefits to me as the reader; there's no incentive for me to read or respond to this letter.

Sample Letter A:

Letter written in 'corporate' style (writer's business name has been changed).

Mrs C Bentley
Promote Your Business Ltd
104 Victoria Avenue
Swanage
BH19 1AS

Dear Mrs Bentley,

I would like to take this opportunity to introduce myself and my company, Huff & Puff Solicitors, to you.

Huff & Puff Solicitors have been established since 1937. We have a large team of professionals covering a wide range of commercial law from employment through to commercial property.

I would be pleased to explain the different services we offer and trust that you will call me if you need our advice and help.

Yours sincerely,

Sample Letter B

Letter re-written in 'personal' style

Dear Mrs Bentley,

One Legal Slip Could Cost You Thousands of Pounds

There are so many different aspects of business where you have to be sure you are acting within the law. This can include employment law, contracts with other businesses and when you are renting or purchasing commercial property. Not doing so can damage your professional image as well as your bank balance.

At Huff & Puff Solicitors we understand how crucial understanding and working within the law is for a business such as yours.

You can be sure that any decisions you make will not expose you to unwelcome litigation when you follow our advice. Our large team of professionals cover a wide range of commercial law from employment through to commercial property.

You are welcome to take advantage of the FREE half-hour consultation we offer to discuss anything that is causing you concern. You are not obliged to take our services following this meeting, although we do hope that the good guidance we offer gives you the confidence to do so.

I look forward to meeting you.

Yours sincerely,

Sample letter B is a rewrite of the letter I received.

Even when you are writing to businesses you should avoid stilted, formal language in your letter, after all you are still writing to a person who has their own aspirations and problems to overcome.

Personally I feel the second version would have got a better response than the first, what do you think?

In the next step in this sequence we take a look at a scientific formula for structuring your sales letter and how to make it easy for your prospect to buy.

Before going on to that, take a look at your existing sales letters. Are they too formal? Are they written from your reader's point of view? Try re-writing them in a more friendly, reader focused style - you may be surprised at the outcome.

STEP 5:
SIMPLE FORMULA FOR
WINNING SALES

OK, we've got the headline and the content sorted. Now we need to think about the structure of your sales message. The good news is there is a formula you can use to make sure your sales letter is as effective as it can be. First off, let's talk about AIDA...

Sales professionals are often taught to use the **AIDA** sequence in their sales presentations.

You may have come across this acronym... it stands for:

Attention

Interest

Desire

Action

Same as with a Sales Presentation, it is crucial for your letter to catch your reader's **Attention**, otherwise it won't be read. And if s/he doesn't read it s/he won't respond. If what you are offering is important to him and you haven't managed to persuade him to read your letter, you have let him down, because he'll never know about what you offer.

Grabbing attention is the role of your headline - covered in step 2 of this guide.

Having got his attention you must keep his **Interest** in what you are writing about, then create a **Desire** to own / receive whatever it is you are offering. And finally get your reader to take **Action**.

If you don't take your reader through the whole of this process it is unlikely you'll get his custom.

I use what I call the '**extended AIDA**' – AIDA-A. The extra 'A' is another 'Attention Mechanism' namely the post script at the end of your letter. It's often your second chance to catch your reader's attention and it should be as compelling and strong as your main headline or opening sentence.

Why Do I Need A PS?

When people receive their post – whether it is personal or business – they often use a subconscious selection process for the order they open and read it in.

The most common 3-step sequence people follow is:

Sort   S/he decides, probably without really thinking about it, the order s/he will open each item. Usually s/he'll open bulky – interesting – packages first because they create curiosity, especially if they are unexpected, followed by any hand-written letters. These are more personal and likely to be from a friend or relation. Next comes the 'official – looking' letters such as bank statements, government correspondence etc. Finally, if at all, the 'junk mail'.

Yes, that's what we call it, isn't it? The marketing letters from people who are trying to catch our attention are often referred to as 'junk mail'. And, whether we like it or not, our sales letters may be regarded in the same way – especially if the person has no interest in what we are writing about because we have not targeted the right people. (See step 1 in this guide on how to find the right people).

Open When a letter is opened research has shown that most people will:

1. Check the name and address to make sure it is addressed correctly to them.

2. Read the headline or the first sentence.

3. If that has attracted their attention sufficiently, the end of the letter is checked to see who it is from and...

4. If there is a P.S. this is read as well. (*There should **always** be a P.S. – it is your second chance to get your reader's attention and entice him to read your letter*).

Read Then the decision is made to either 'bin the letter' or read it.

It is your job to make sure your letter is read, and not binned, by getting every possible aspect of it right so your targeted audience responds in the way you want them to.

By the way, 'gimmicky' bulk mail only works *if* the recipient is interested in your offer and it is appropriate to what you supply. No amount of clever 'promotional gifts or inserts' creates a response where there is no interest or desire. That's where targeting your audience makes a real difference.

Make Your Offer Irresistible

Having grabbed the reader's attention with your brilliantly written headline/opening sentence the next step is to keep their interest. Make sure you follow up the headline with something that encourages them to read on.

As you write your letter you must aim to get your reader excited about your offer – that's where the information about it, how it's been used by others and their testimonials – does some of the work for you.

You must 'paint the picture' so your reader sees himself using your product or getting the result your service promises. Then...

Tell Them What To Do Next...

Now you have got your reader keyed up with your letter and offer – don't let him down. Tell him the action he needs to take, the next step he must follow so he can have the promised results for himself.

Don't assume he will figure out he can phone, write or send an email to you. He is a busy person – make it as easy as possible for him. Tell him to phone the 0800 number; tell him to complete the request / enquiry form (never call it an order form by the way) or tell him to visit your website or send an email NOW!

Emphasise the urgency of taking the next step whilst it is fresh in his mind. If he thinks "I'll do that later" it won't happen. Chances are your letter and response mechanism will get buried under all the other things vying for his attention every day.

Make it Easy for Your Prospect

Whenever we purchase something we 'take a risk' that what we are buying will do what we want or give us the result we are looking for.

And, although we don't vocalise it, the question we are asking is "are we getting value for our money, will I regret this purchase?"

Because you believe in your service or product you would be quick to reassure your customer "Yes, you get exactly what I'm promising". You would do your best to remove any doubt from his mind.

One way you can do this in your letter is by using 'risk-reversal' – effectively giving your customer reassurance and your guarantee 'up-front'.

By telling your customer you give, for example, a 100% money-back guarantee you are taking the risk off his shoulders, giving him the confidence and peace of mind to go ahead.

I was explaining this to a client of mine who is a business coach. She was very concerned about giving a money-back guarantee and in fact said she found it 'very scary'.

When I asked her what she would do if a client of hers was unhappy with her service, would she give them a refund or say "tough!" she quickly responded she wouldn't want the client to be unhappy and would refund immediately.

"Well, where's the difference?" I asked "As an ethical business woman you would treat your client decently, why not tell people at the beginning so they are reassured, rather than 'crossing that bridge' if you come to it?"

Many businesses are concerned about giving guarantees because they think people will take advantage. Most people genuinely want to do business and gain the advantage you are describing. Provided your service or product <u>does</u> perform as you have claimed then your customer will be happy and unlikely to ask for a refund.

Experience has shown the attrition rate when some sort of guarantee is offered rarely reaches even 5%. So, if offering a risk-reversal guarantee increases your results by, let's say, 45% then, even if you do have an unexpected 5% attrition, you have still gained 40% you wouldn't have had without the guarantee.

In the next step in this sequence - your penultimate step - I reveal the 8 Elements of a

Winning Sales Letter.

Meantime, let me ask... how easy do you make it for your prospect to buy? Do you have a guarantee that gives peace of mind? If not, what could you offer that makes you stand out from your competitors?

Notes:

STEP 6:
8 MUST-HAVE ELEMENTS FOR
SALES-GENERATING LETTERS...

In the last step we began to look at the structure of your sales letter, starting with the AIDA-A formula.

In this section, I'm expanding on that AIDA-A sequence. Including these 8 elements in your letter (each tie in with AIDA-A), means you boost the potential response your letter gets:

1. **Headline** – I can't emphasise enough how important it is to spend the majority of your time on this. It is the ATTENTION part of the AIDA-A acronym. As previously mentioned, aim to write as close to 100 headlines as you can. Include power response words that have proven to be key to getting a positive reaction from readers.

2. **Promise** - follow up on what you promised in the headline to keep your reader's interest. If you promised some key information, tell them what it is. If your headline offered a critical report – tell them what the report contains and how it can help them. This keeps your reader's INTEREST.

3. **Offer** - Describe exactly what you are offering,

what it does for them, how they benefit - the results they receive. If there are a number of steps to a process describe exactly what you are going to do for them – start to create their DESIRE.

4. **Testimonial** – people respond to other people's experiences and recommendations. The human nature of 'I want that too!' comes into play. Make sure your testimonials are descriptive and identify the problem the person had or the result they wanted and the solution / outcome your product or service provided (mentioned in step 3). This keeps your reader's DESIRE high. He wants to know more.

5. **Lose** – It is your job to make sure your reader cannot possibly ignore your offer. You have to make absolutely sure he understands <u>exactly</u> how much less his life will be if he does not respond to your valuable proposition. You would be harming him by not doing everything possible to clearly show the loss he would experience. So tell him what he loses if he doesn't respond. How he will miss out on key benefits or results, how his life will never be the same again...

OK, so I'm exaggerating, but I'm sure you get the picture ☺. People buy on emotions and then use logic to justify their decisions. You need to appeal to your reader's emotional wants / desires – the detail you provide helps him justify the logic of buying from you.

If we didn't buy on emotion, people would never

buy expensive cars, designer clothes or larger houses. After all a small, cheap car gets you from A to B, just as a more expensive car would. "Ah, but" I sometimes hear "it isn't as comfortable, reliable etc."

That's our logic justifying the emotion of owning and being seen in a high status, luxurious car rather than an old rusty tin-can.

This is still part of your reader's DESIRE – his desire not to lose what you have already created an interest in.

So, having 'depressed' your reader with what he might lose if he doesn't take your offer, now you must ...

6. **Repeat the benefits** – increase your prospect's desire even more to own or experience your service / product. Get your reader excited about what he can expect.

   And then...

7. **Action** – tell him <u>exactly</u> what to do now. Tell him to send the completed request form in the envelope provided. Tell him to call the Freephone number and place his request NOW. Tell him to send the email confirming his interest. Don't let him 'cool off' by not leading him through the steps he needs to take immediately.

   Many people completely forget to include this element in their sales letters, it's the same as if a

Sales Person gave a fantastic presentation and then left without asking for the order! A complete waste of time. Both the Sales Person and the prospect's. Don't waste your reader's time; if your letter has done its job so far and your prospect has invested his time reading it, don't you think he'd like to know how to take up your offer?

8. And finally add the **P.S.** – the final part of the AIDA-A acronym and, effectively, your second headline. Having spent so much time preparing your main headline you have probably discovered your second strongest – and that is likely to be a natural P.S. The purpose of your P.S. is to draw the reader into your letter, so it too should be compelling.

In the final step in this sequence, I reveal how to make sure you do not waste your marketing budget.

Meantime - check you've got each of these elements in your winning sales letters.

STEP 7:
HOW TO BE CONFIDENT OF YOUR MARKETING ROI

Do me a favour, will you?

Please, do not take any of the marketing and copywriting advice you get, whether it is from me or someone else, at face value.

All the advice you receive can certainly point you in the right direction; give you ideas on how to make your marketing work more effectively; tell you what has worked for other businesses in the past and works currently, but no-one knows your business and your prospective customers as intimately as you do.

Sure - take all this knowledge on board, but do so with a 'pinch of salt' and test the ideas, test the letters, test the promotions - whatever marketing activity you decide to use please test it before you throw your whole marketing budget into the pot! Only by testing are you sure you are investing your money wisely.

Allocate a good proportion of your marketing budget for testing, around 20%. Invest this sum by sending your test letters to a small portion of your database. Then, when you have a measured response, you can be more confident about sending out to a larger portion of your list.

The challenge we all have is to understand we see things from our own, personal perspective – and so does everyone else - that's why testing is crucial. It means a headline; offer or guarantee you feel extremely confident about can still bomb because it does not appeal to your prospects.

How Reliable Is Your Judgement?

To demonstrate this further take a look at these samples and select the headlines that appeal to you. Then, without letting anyone see your choice, ask a few other people to do the same.

Finally compare your selections with the results at the end of this section showing the headlines that got the best response.

a)   Advert for a course in English:

"The Man Who Simplified English"

"Do You Make These Mistakes in English?"

b)   Advert for a Book

"How to Win Friends and Influence People"

"How to Ruin Your Marriage in the Quickest Possible Way"

c)   Insurance Company

"Retirement Income Plan"

"What Would Become of Your Wife If Something Happened to You?"

d) Property Letting Management Agency

"Quality, Professional Letting Management"

"Your Investment in *<development>* is Probably Worth More Than You Think..."

What To Test

There are more things to test in a sales letter than you might expect. Here are some suggestions of what to test...

- Headline; one against another
- Sub heading content
- Opening paragraph content
- Offer; one price against another
- Offer; different product or service offers
- Letter length: short versus long
- Adding a lift letter
- With / without sample (if appropriate)
- Letter layout; paragraph lengths, subheads, with / without photos
- With/without glossy brochure
- Envelopes – size/printed/plain/window
- Stamps v franking
- Response mechanism; order form v telephone ordering v online ordering

Do remember – only test one element at a time. If you make too many changes you won't know which modification has generated an increase - or decrease - in response.

On a web sales page you can test different elements of your sales message at the same time - know as multi-variate testing - and check your website statistics for the number of visitors and conversions to find out what works best for you. This does speed up the testing process.

How To Test & Monitor Results

Split testing allows you to establish which is the most successful of your letters more quickly. The system most frequently used is an A/B split test where 2 versions of the same letter (with just one difference, e.g. different headlines) are sent out at the same time. One letter goes to half your list and the 2nd letter goes to the other half.

To make sure you know which version of your letter has generated the highest response code the response mechanism in each letter.

The code can be a Dept reference in the address or a printed code on a response form or a specific 0800 number that matches that version of the letter.

Change the reference code for your letter every time you make an alteration – no matter how small. And keep a record of what has been changed; sometimes changes to your letter can drop response and you need to know what to change back before testing your next alteration.

Using a unique code for each version means you'll

always know <u>exactly why</u> your response dropped or increased.

For example you could use a code, similar to this, as part of the postal address:

Dept **ST236a**

ST – represents the campaign timing e.g. Summer Time

23 – represents the week number when the letter was sent

6 – is the offer or product

a – is the version of the letter

The letter (a) would be changed whenever a modification is made, no matter how small. So, in this case, the second version would be 6b.

When you have a 'winning formula' don't be complacent. Monitor all your results so you know the trend and continue testing to find an even better sales or lead generating letter.

How Reliable Was Your Judgement? - *Results*

Compare your choice to what the marketing people discovered when they tested these headlines:

a)   Advert for English course:

"The Man Who Simplified English"

**   "Do You Make These Mistakes in English?"   **

The second headline produced nearly **three times more sales** than the first generated.

b)   Advert for a Book

**   "How to Win Friends and Influence People" **

"How to Ruin Your Marriage in the Quickest Possible Way"

This book, which is well known throughout the world, was written by Dale Carnegie and incorporated into his training courses. The 'How to Win' headline **out-pulled** the other by nearly **250%**

---

c)   Insurance Company

**   "Retirement Income Plan"   **

"What Would Become of Your Wife If Something Happened to You?"

The first headline **increased response** over the second by **nearly 500%**

---

d)   Property Letting Management Agency

"Quality, Professional Letting Management"

** **"Your Investment in *<development>* is Probably Worth More Than You Think..."** **

The second headline, used on a direct-response letter, created a massive 44.2% response, 63.16% of which took out a management agreement with the letting agent.

No-one's selection is wrong – everyone chooses what appeals to them.

Your job is to find the combination of headline, offer and guarantee that attracts the highest number of people in your target market.

This is the final step in this Pocket Guide.

I'm curious to know, how helpful was this guide to you? Did you get some useful tips or were they just a load of re-hashed common sense stuff you already knew? Pop your thoughts in an email to me at success@carolbentley.com.

And tell me, what's your toughest challenge in marketing your business right now and what sort of help do you need?

Notes:

OTHER RESOURCES

More on Copywriting Techniques...

The steps in this guide are a distillation of the more extensive techniques revealed in my book **'I Want To Buy Your Product.. Have You Sent Me A Letter Yet?'**

The 18 chapters in that book are packed with a professional copywriter's insights. Inside you'll discover:

- The <u>right language</u> to cut through communication barriers. Discover how to connect with **all of your** readers - not just the normal 20% - 30%.

- <u>79 'Attention' words and phrases</u> to draw your readers in. More proven power words you can use to create your compelling headlines.

- <u>36 Appeals</u> to attract responses. When your headline and offer satisfy one or more of these appeals your letter hits the 'hot-spot' for the highest proportion of your readers and so creates awesome response and results.

- <u>How to design a responsive order form</u>. The 'order form' is considered by many copywriters to be the most important part of any package sent out. **An ill-designed response form can kill the sale.** Discover how to design your order form to encourage your prospect to buy.

- <u>How to handle 'writer's block'</u>. Three different

methods to 'kick-start' your writing. Which one works best for you?

- <u>9 biggest mistakes</u> people make <u>in newsletters</u> - and how to avoid them.

- <u>3 Checklists</u>:

  - Preparing to Write - <u>27 questions</u> to make sure you've got everything you need to hand;

  - Your sales letter - <u>20 key points</u>, match these to make your sales letter completely irresistible;

  - Response form design - these <u>31 design elements</u> keep you on track.

Numerous business people have already used these simple to follow techniques to gain massive increases in response to their sales letters:

"Well, having purchased your book at the event, we swiftly put some of your ideas into practice. Our previous mailing letter went in the bin, and a refreshed version was generated. It is fair to say that the response level we now get has vastly increased. Not only in terms of immediate response, but also from those who have obviously retained our information and called some months later. We look back at our previous attempt and cringe."

Andy Littlecott
Buckfield Environmental (Asbestos Removal)

"Outstanding! It shows you an easy way to transform mediocre letters to explosive letters - the kind that get noticed, get read, get sales!"

Dr. Joe Vitale,
Author of "The Attractor Factor"... www.mrfire.com

"Thanks again for the advice. I never dreamed that I'd journey so far on the back of one book! They say excellence = expectation + 1. I think you've already delivered expectation + 101"

David Bowen

The book can be purchased through Amazon & good bookstores or direct from me online at **www.carolbentley.com/offer**

Proven Marketing Tactics

In '**Beat The Recession: Proven Marketing Tactics**' I reveal 139 easy to read and implement marketing tactics:

- 27 Direct Marketing Insights Boost Your Sales Results
- 37 Articles Reveal Valuable Business Resources & Show How To Save Your Time
- 28 Writing Tips To Make Your Sales Letters Zing
- 11 Inspirational Pearls of Wisdom Designed to Motivate You
- 13 Web Marketing Tips Expand Your Global Reach

Plus...

- 19 Added Value Articles Contributed by 10 Business Professionals and Authors
- Download links for 14 gifts including:
  - Phrases That Grab Attention
  - Crafting Headlines MindMap
  - Direct Mail Secrets
  - Marketing with eNewsletters

- Can LinkedIn Increase Your Sales?
- Service Sellers Master Course
- Make Your Price Sell
- Web Marketing Strategy Mindmaps
- Powerful Interview Transcripts

and other gems scattered throughout the book...

Business owners are already benefiting from the marketing gems in this book:

This is truly the best value I've EVER had in the written word. With 24 years business experience, I'm invigorated by the strategies that are given Step by Step.

*This book is a must buy for any entrepreneur. One word of warning... have a pen, pencil and laptop close by, there are **hundreds of references** that you will want to explore and all **Free of Charge** 'yippee do day'.*

*Where did you get all that gelignite information from? BEST buy EVER - we've **just experienced our best February ever in the middle of a recession!** Well Done Carol.*

William Little MD
Cleaning Doctor 18th March 2009

"I've studied your book and used the knowledge gained to write many letters to my existing customers and as a result, I am getting more repeat work from my existing carpet & upholstery cleaning customers. **I am achieving about 30% more results** from using these techniques."

Gerwyn Jones

"Good practical and usable stuff with a **down to earth no BS approach**.

But let's not underestimate the enormity of going from ground zero to a truly effective copywriter. There are probably a handful of great copywriters in this country.

My strategy is to be a bit better than most out there who don't use or can't afford these few stars!"

Graham Rowan
National Nutrition Clinic, Richmond, Surrey

This book is also available through Amazon and good bookstores or you can purchase direct from **www.bentleybtr.com**

Books purchased online direct from me are personally signed and come with a FREE PDF version of the book to keep on your computer desktop for instant reference.

THE ALTERNATIVE...

If, having read this Pocket Guide, you've decided you do not have the time - *or perhaps inclination* - to write your own sales and marketing material you can engage a professional to create your copy for you.

Use your knowledge of the principles revealed in this guide to make sure the material delivered is up to the required standard for the job.

If you have not hired a copywriter before use the following quick guide to make sure you find the right professional for you...

How to Select Your Ideal Copywriter - 9 Points to Consider

Check the person you choose to write your sales-generating letter is the professional you want and can deliver the material you need within your timescale and budget – here's the minimum to look for...

- **Before seeking your copywriter**, decide what you want written. Do you want...

  - o A powerful sales letter?
  - o A company brochure?
  - o A press release?
  - o Feature articles?
  - o Reports or 'white-papers'?
  - o Promotional tips booklet /guide?
  - o Copy for a website?
  - o An email marketing campaign?
  - o Advertising copy?
  - o A staff handbook?
  - o A procedures manual?
  - o A technical guide?
  - o Catalogue copy?

  Many of these writing activities need different skills and approaches. When you've decided what you want produced you can look for someone who has experience in that particular discipline.

  For example, if you want a sales / marketing letter look for a professional who has experience in direct response copywriting. (This is a specialised skill that many copywriters do not have).

- **Is s/he professional?** By that I mean does s/he take the trouble to ask questions about your business, your goals and, if you are looking for a sales letter, does s/he ask about your offer and what other marketing you've already done and the response you got?

Look for a copywriter who asks you to complete a fact-gathering questionnaire.

- And talking of professionalism, **does s/he supply a contract and terms of business** so you know exactly what to expect and what s/he is agreeing to do for you?

- **Does s/he have a good reputation?** Do you know their work? Have you heard good things about the material s/he has produced for other businesses? Does their style match yours?

- **How does s/he charge?** By the hour; by the page or number of words; or does s/he give a project charge before starting?

Be careful.

Writing is creative work.

It takes time to craft the documents you want, especially if it is a sales letter or marketing piece. Charges by the hour can mount up and storm past your budget before you realise it.

And be cautious about restricting the number of pages or words you want someone to write - unless it is a requirement for the project - for example when writing an article for a publication that has to be a specific length.

That would be like putting a gag on your best sales person after they've just got started.

- **Is the copywriter** you've chosen **prepared to quote a price for the project**(and stick to it), to make budgeting easier for you? Dependent upon the work you are asking for you may be able to negotiate a lower initial fee with a commission on results achieved.

Beware - if the fees are very low, ask yourself why?

- **Is s/he easy to work with?** You want someone you can talk to; someone who matches your enthusiasm for your product or service; someone who is genuinely interested in what you provide and what you want to achieve; someone who listens and takes on board your ideas.

And you want a copywriter who is willing to explain why s/he has taken a particular approach and why s/he thinks it will work for you.

- **Does s/he research your project?** Obviously you need to provide as much material, information, insights and supporting documentation as you can. But the mark of a true professional is the copywriter who goes that extra mile by doing their own research to enhance what you've supplied.

- **Is s/he reliable?** Does s/he meet deadlines, deliver on time? There's no point having a good copywriter if s/he constantly misses deadlines. That's particularly important when you are sending out offers with a specific offer period or geared to anniversaries or seasons.

Carol Bentley does not write technical manuals, although she has developed 'how-to' computer training manuals as part of her earlier career. Carol's speciality is writing direct response sales and marketing material, white papers and tips guides for businesses to use as part of their marketing strategy.

Details of the copywriting services Carol offers are described at **www.carolbentley.com**

Need a Conference Speaker?

Want to share these sales and marketing techniques with your staff or colleagues? Engage Carol Bentley as a speaker at your next event.

Or organise an in-house workshop and take advantage of Carol's 20+ years as a computer skills trainer and her experience as an ex-Dale Carnegie Instructor (prior to specialising in B2B copywriting) to enhance your team's sales writing techniques.

I recently attended a seminar Carol Bentley was running and to say the very least I was impressed. Not only is Carol a very nice person, but her approach was both impeccable and plausible. Throughout the seminar the delegate's interest was maintained due to the straight forward and understandable delivery of Carol's presentation, and she was able to get a tremendous amount of participation during the day because of her good humour and her ability to take time to understand people's individual requirements.

In this day and age it is all too easy to complain when you pay for a service and get sub standard results, but any one who has met and heard Carol will know that consistently she delivers the goods.

Nigel Tucker, Director. Otterdene Studio Ltd

Call **0800 015 5515** (UK freephone); outside UK: +44 1929 423411 or email **success@carolbentley.com**

Lightning Source UK Ltd.
Milton Keynes UK
26 November 2009

146743UK00001B/9/P